Let It Go

Burn, Bury, Rip, Repeat

AND MAKE WAY FOR WHAT MAKES YOU
HEALTHIER, HAPPIER, WEALTHIER, WISER.

BY JOANNA ARETTAM

Red Wheel
Boston, MA / York Beach, ME

First published in 2003 by
Red Wheel/Weiser, LLC
York Beach, ME
With offices at:
368 Congress Street
Boston, MA 02210
www.redwheelweiser.com

ISBN 1-59003-026-5

Typeset in Berthold Akzidenz Grotesk, Giddyup, Gill Sans, Myriad, Sackers, Savoye,
and The Sans.

Printed in The United States of America
PC

09   08   07   06   05   04   03   02
 8   7   6   5   4   3   2   1

The paper used in this publication meets the minimum requirements of the American
National Standard for Information Sciences—Permanence of Paper for Printed Library
Materials Z39.48-1992 (R1997).

TABLE OF CONTENTS
TABLE OF CONTENTS

The practices suggested in this book are intended as transformational tools for adults. When we suggest shredding, flushing, burying, or burning the workbook pages, we are not advocating irresponsible or unecological practices. Paper is made from cellulose, a natural plant fiber. The cellulose in tiny pieces of paper released into an open field will be rapidly reclaimed by the earth, just as on a beach, it will be broken down by the salt water and ultraviolet light. This is equally true if you bury or flush your pages. If you burn them, please do so carefully, in a fireplace or sturdy earthen vessel indoors, and away from dry shrubbery outdoors; do not wear loose clothing when you work with fire. This is not a book for children.

How to Give Up Your Hair Shirt for a Cashmere Wrap

"Turn your stumbling blocks
into stepping stones."
—Anonymous

Are you feeling bummed out?

Ticked off?
Hemmed in?
Tied down?
Choked up?

Is that hair shirt getting itchy?

Are you suffocating under **heavy** covers?

You know the feelings I'm talking about—the ones you reflexively hold close to yourself the way a toddler clings to a fuzzy blanket. The difference between the toddler's binky and your own is that the former is a soft fabric woven in a comforting color and design, and the latter is a spiky, knotted mass of fear, anger, resentment, unhappiness—you name it—woven with recurring, often destructive, patterns.

Nothing comforting there! And you've been clutching that emotional blanket for years.

You're not alone. We all become attached to something abrasively familiar. "Better the enemy you know than the one you don't," my grandmother used to say. Well, it's time to meet your psychic, internal foes and eliminate them from your life.

Our mantra, and our **modus operandi,** is

Let it Go.

Know What You Want to Let Go

Part One of this book is to help you identify the enemies, because you can't eliminate them if you don't know what they are. Fear, anger, mistrust, we'll find out what you're holding onto. Once you learn to recognize the uncomfortable threads in your emotional blanket, you can pull them out one by one. When they're gone, that scratchy fabric will be transformed into a radiant mantle of calm, the psychic equivalent of a soft, cashmere wrap.

Change it into something new. Transformation is the theme of Part Two. Here we turn to the four elements—fire, water, air, earth—and to rituals and contemplative actions that allow you to alter your issues and render them harmless before releasing them forever.

Key to this transformation is writing your intent, for the simple act of acknowledging what you want to change reinforces your will and sets in motion the action that will make it so. At the back of the section you'll find Contracts for Transformation—ritual pages for you to write on before transforming them.

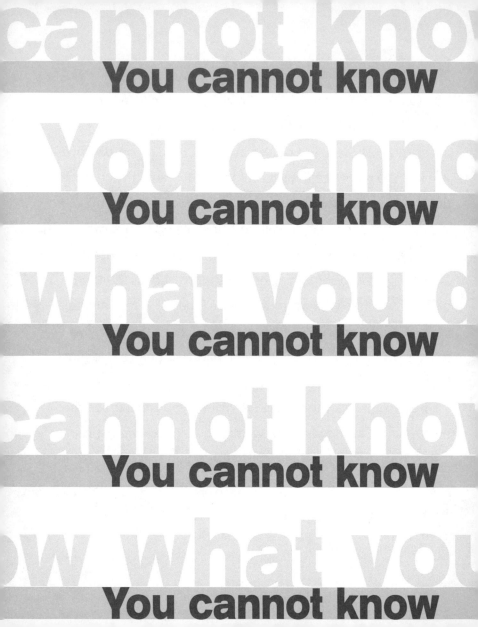

what you do not feel.

– Marya Mannes, **They**

what you do not feel.

– Marya Mannes, **They**

what you do not feel.

– Marya Mannes, **They**

what you do not feel.

– Marya Mannes, **They**

what you do not feel.

For instance, if anger is one of your issues, write a list of the things that make you see red. Bury the contract in a pot with loamy soil; then, into that small vessel of earth place the seeds or bulb of a plant that will grow to yield a brilliant crimson flower. It's much more civilized than having a tantrum.

It's even more than an assuaging gardening interlude. It's a physically transformative act that allows you to take control and make change in your life. Is there a better way to see red than in the petals of a flower you have cultivated yourself?

Let It Go! offers many such ideas for transformation and change (and acknowledges that some of the most powerful rituals will spring from your own intuition). The idea, of course, is to let go of the negative emotions that have held you back so that you can make way for new, affirmative energies that attract and welcome what you want to have—and who you want to be.

Do unto **yourself** as you would do unto **others.**

—Anonymous

As soon as you trust yourself,
you will know how to live.

—Goethe

part one

What's Holding You Back?

No one has a problem with feeling too happy.

You really can't be overwhelmed with gratitude or peacefulness because you naturally disperse the excess—through good will and good deeds, or just through a good mood that elevates you and surrounds you with what others perceive as good vibes. Even negative emotions can be a good thing if you can peel back that first layer of pain and listen to what they have to say. Dissatisfaction may spur you to do better, for instance; suspicion, to get to the truth.

On the other hand, chronic negative emotions are not a good thing. They ooze out as bad vibes, but they also cram themselves into every available emotional cell until you feel as if you could explode from the pain (and sometimes do).

{
Anger makes
dull men
[and women]
witty,
but it keeps
them poor.
}

–Queen Elizabeth I

Your emotions are holding you back if they don't allow you to see beyond them. If you're always dissatisfied, nothing you do will make a difference. If you hate your body, how can you love yourself? Or someone else?

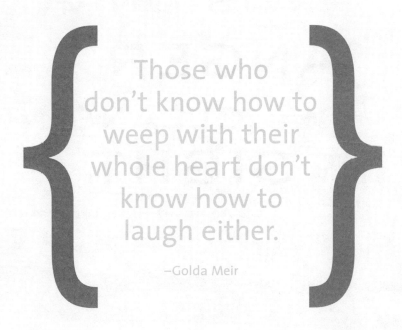

{ Those who don't know how to weep with their whole heart don't know how to laugh either. }

−Golda Meir

My VISIONARY ANGER CLEANSING my SIGHT.

–Adrienne Rich, The Stranger

Your emotions are holding you back if they make you feel sick. They're holding you back if you find yourself trying to stuff them down with food, exhale them as smoke, wash them away with alcohol, or deny them altogether by getting high.

As you begin to contemplate what's been holding you back, think about the blanket you've been clutching. Emotional blankets are woven with threads in five major "colors." Let's call them: anger, fear, hate, mistrust, and unhappiness. Those threads in turn have many subtle tints and tones (see the following pages). A blanket of loneliness, for instance, may incorporate a rainbow of negative feelings: frustration, anxiety, low self image, mistrust, and disappointment, while a blanket of sadness may be monochromatic, a study in "blue" so to speak, with many shades of unhappiness, from dissatisfaction with a job, to lack of fulfillment in a relationship, to sorrow at how important situations in your life have been resolved, to an inability to acknowledge or appreciate the good things that have come your way.

NEVER build a case against YOURSELF

−Robert Rowbottom

This book does not have all the answers you need, but it will tap the one person who does: You. Read with your heart as well as your mind. And give your inner voice the opportunity to respond. Together you'll begin to identify the issues that are holding you back, and together we will let them go.

START

Nothing can bring you peace but yourself.

—Ralph Waldo Emerson

Recognize Any of These?

Given the vibrant tonalities of life, emotions are rarely black or white. So while you may not feel consumed by deep sorrow or explosive rage—at least not for long—you may find that more subtle versions, such as *disappointment* or *anxiety*, have grayed and flattened your life over time. Indeed, it's far easier to recognize the extreme version of an emotion—and to want to get rid of it—than to identify a debilitating subtlety that has insinuated itself as constant companion. Following are the words I've used to express a range of sentiments within the five categories, as well as their more-or-less opposites. It's by no means complete, so feel free to add your own words to this page. Refer to it when you're having trouble figuring out what it is you really feel and want to let go of and what you'd like to replace it with instead.

No emotion is the final one.

—Jeanette Winterson,
Oranges Are Not the Only Fruit

ANGER CALM

impatience	easefulness
frustration	acceptance
blame	praise
tension	tranquility
rage	release without the drama

_____ _____

_____ _____

_____ _____

_____ _____

_____ _____

FEAR COURAGE

anxiety · relief

insecurity · self-esteem

jealousy · pleasure at another's good fortune

panic · centeredness

terror · coolheaded response to a threat

_____ · _____

_____ · _____

_____ · _____

_____ · _____

HATE LOVE

· ·

dislike	affection
low self-esteem	self-respect
annoyance	compassion
selfishness	altruism
spite	spirituality

_____   _____

_____   _____

_____   _____

_____   _____

_____   _____

MISTRUST TRUST

doubt   inquisitiveness

dishonesty   generosity

suspicion   truthfulness

stubbornness   intuition

inability to accept   openness

_____   _____

_____   _____

_____   _____

_____   _____

_____   _____

UNHAPPINESS HAPPINESS

dissatisfaction	contentment
disappointment	pleasure
despair	optimism
sadness	joy
grief	ecstacy

_____

_____

_____

_____

_____

Is Anger Holding You Back?

Anger is power. Tempered with wisdom, it can move mountains. Americans of all stripes have freedom today not just because a handful of leaders signed it into being but because heroic individuals, followed by committed groups, channeled their anger into such important work as the Civil Rights Movement, Women's Liberation, and Lesbian and Gay Rights. This works individually, too. When Sheila H., a ferociously can-do personality, was stuck in a taxi amid a skein of honking cars, she got ticked off. But instead of stewing, she got out and directed traffic around the obstruction. When the cars started rolling, she jumped back into the taxi to a round of grateful waves and toots. The point is to express your negative feeling in a constructive way before it explodes in destructive fury—and what's communication but the verbal form of directing traffic?

Anger is holding you back if you just sit there and lean on the horn. Anger is your last nerve permanently on its last nerve.

Are blow ups my primary means of communication?

Are headaches and tense muscles my norm?

Are strangers offended by my rudeness?

Do colleagues hold their breath around me?

Are the people I love afraid of me?

Ask yourself: (Write your own questions here.)

_____

_____

_____

_____

_____

_____

"I have not ceased being fearful, but I have ceased to let fear control me," writes novelist Erica Jong. " I have accepted fear as a part of life, specifically the fear of change, the fear of the unknown, and I have gone ahead despite the pounding in the heart that says: turn back, turn back, you'll die if you venture too far."

Is Fear Holding You Back?

Fear is good! It's how we as a species—actually, all species—have survived. Without fear we might have walked blissfully into a galloping herd of buffalo back when we were walking on all fours and never gotten to be humans at all. Fortunately we have this marvelous instinct that allows our auto-pilot, the autonomic nervous system, to take over. Car coming? Without thinking about it, we dash out of the way fueled by adrenaline, just as our ancestors did with those buffalo.

The world can be a scary place, especially now that terrorism tops the evening news reports. Unfortunately sensationalism sells, so you begin to feel as if you're under siege. And that's at home in the recliner! Look, you do have to make sure things are right in your corner of the universe—checking the stove, locking the door, keeping to the speed limit, watching your cholesterol, whatever—but once you do, just head out, live your life, and expect to return home that evening.

Fear is holding you back when every decision is made to avoid something you don't want to face, rather than to encounter something you do. It's holding you back when the "fight or flight" mechanism, which is meant to kick in for an emergency, remains in the permanent "on" position resulting in constant, debilitating anxiety. And it shows itself in relationships when jealousy or insecurity, rather than joy or passion, are the predominant emotions.

Do I plan my schedule around avoiding people I don't want to see, situations I don't want to deal with?

If I think about it, would I realize that I rarely make a full inhalation or exhalation, breathing instead in a shallow, unrelaxed way?

Do family and friends make allowances for (or have difficulty dealing with) my timidities and apprehensions?

Am I possessive in relationships?

Am I in a possessive relationship?

Ask yourself: (Write your own questions here.)

_____

_____

_____

_____

_____

Is Hate Holding You Back?

Hate is another mountain mover because it propels you into action. Hate how your life is going? Well, that's a motivation to change things, isn't it? The bad hate is the constant negativity that saps your good energy. You hate your ex. You hate your ex's new spouse. You hate the person who got the job you wanted. You hate your job. No wonder you're bummed out.

Then there's the more mundane expression of loathing that you hear, and perhaps use, in conversation all the time: I hate my thighs. I hate that song. I can't stand that dress. I hate the way you leave your socks on the floor. Eventually you start to really loathe those mundane situations. And it's hard to let the good stuff into port when bitterness and annoyance are docked at every pier.

Hate, or some version of it, is holding you back if annoyance is your response to most situations. It's holding you back if you find something wrong with everything.

Or as Indira Ghandi said simply, "You cannot shake hands with a clenched fist."

Is getting even my way of responding to a situation?

When was the last time I did something nice for someone?

Do I like myself? Whom do I like?

Am I hoarding food or emotions or things?

Have I made room in my heart for the spirit?

Ask yourself: (Write your own questions here.)

_____

_____

_____

_____

_____

Is Mistrust Holding You Back?

There's that one-liner: It's not paranoia if someone is out to get you. Irony, a witty and usually healthy form of mistrust, helps us put things in perspective, even laugh about them. Out at the extremes, though, there's a chasm between blind and unwarranted faith ("Trust me on this," says the con man—and you do) and the inability to accept even the most heartfelt offerings of generosity or affection.

Irony is a great tool for a comic, and skepticism is a great quality for a journalist, just as suspicion is for a detective, as persistence is for a researcher. Like the hammer and chisels that allow a sculptor to realize a figure from a block of marble, these are the emotions that help us get to the truth. Overworked, however, they're bitterness, intolerance, paranoia, and stubbornness, the sledgehammer that smashes that figure to pieces.

Mistrust is holding you back if you suspect the motives or actions in every relationship. If your every move is marked by second guessing. If you feel that showing your true self will automatically invite disaster.

Can I give freely of my feelings?

Of my material possessions?

Do I look forward to new situations where I can meet people and make friends? Have I been called stubborn (OK, pigheaded) by the people who know me best? Can I accept kindness?

Do I listen to my inner voice?

Ask yourself: (Write your own questions here.)

_____

_____

_____

_____

_____

FEELINGS CHANGE FACTS.

—PHYLLIS BOTTOME,
THE LIFE LINE

Is Unhappiness Holding You Back?

Shelter, food, clothing, and reliable transportation fulfill basic human needs. Surely that's why fire and the wheel made an appearance so early in the existence of homo and femina sapiens. It is hard to be happy when you're shivering out in the cold with nowhere to go and no way to get there. But the ideas of status and perfection have created an impossible paradox: No matter how much you have, you want more. And you won't be happy until you get it. If I could just get into a size six I'd really be happy. As soon as I get my dream house I'll be happy. All I need is that Gucci wardrobe/super-size SUV/face lift/hair transplant/corner office/vacation home/platinum bracelet/platinum credit card/trophy wife I'll be happy. Please, please, can I have a pony?

To be sure, there is real unhappiness in life. Grief is an appropriate and necessary response to tragedy—loss of a loved one, a diagnosis of grave illness for you or someone you love, even the loss of a job if you are the sole support of yourself or others. In situations like those, you must mourn. Have a good cry. Seek appropriate professional help, whether it be a grief counselor, medical help or unemployment benefits. And then find the way to Let it Go (because living with grief will kill you).

Unhappiness is holding you back if your well-being is pegged to anything outside yourself, whether it's material possessions or someone's opinion of you. It's holding you back if you're so comfortable with disappointment you don't think to question it.

OH, THE GOOD OLD TIMES WHEN WE WERE SO UNHAPPY!

—FRENCH SAYING

When was the last time I was happy?

What made me happy then?

Is it easier to feel sad than to change my attitude?

Can I find pleasure in art or music?

What makes me laugh?

What am I grateful for?

Ask yourself: (Write your own questions here.)

_____

_____

_____

_____

_____

Make the most of yourself,
for that is all there is to you.
Make the most of yourself,
for that is all there is to you.

**Make the most of yourself,
for that is all there is to you.**

–Ralph Waldo Emerson

Make the most of yourself,
for that is all there is to you.
Make the most of yourself,
for that is all there is to you.
Make the most of yourself,
for that is all there is to you.
Make the most of yourself,

Learning to Untangle the Threads

Each blanket is a unique fabric. By recognizing the emotions that hold you back—and, equally important, the ways they interact in specific situations—you can begin to unravel the weave of your particular negativity. Here are a few examples:

FAILURE

Not achieving the personal or professional success you seek can be a crushing blow. You may feel anger: *They don't get it.* Or fear: *What do I do now?* Your may also feel unhappiness: *Why me?* Mistrust: *What was I thinking?* And some degree of hate, whether directed inward, as in *I'm so stupid.* Or outward, as in *I'll show them.* Fine, acknowledge those feelings. You have to show them to know them. In Part Two of this book, you will let them go. But keep this in mind: "Failure is just a way for our lives to show us we're moving in the wrong direction, that we should try something different," says Oprah Winfrey. (You think her path to success was a smooth, one-way track to the top?)

LOSS

You can lose everything from a treasured piece of jewelry to a long-time job to a loved one. Surprisingly, the emotions for loss are fairly consistent (though certainly different in degree). There's anger: *How could this happen to me?* Fear: *How will I get through this? What do I do now?* Hate, usually in the form of blame: *Someone's going to pay for this!* Unhappiness: *I want to die. I want a cigarette. Where are the donuts?* Feel those feelings. Ask those questions (but ix-nay on the cigarettes and go easy on the donuts). It's important to recognize that cycles continue around you despite your time-stopping loss. The sun rises and sets. The stars come out. Wounded as you are, your heart keeps beating and your chest rises and falls with your breath. Acknowledge these cycles, as well as the abundance in your life, as you begin to relinquish the pain of your loss.

SELF-ESTEEM ISSUES

If attractiveness were measured only by slim hips and big breasts, or by full heads of hair and big penises, we would be a sorely lopsided species. Most of the time you know that. The people you know and love may not have the airbrushed perfection of Hollywood or *Vogue*, but they are pretty close to perfect to you—and you to them. So when frustration, insecurity, jealousy, dissatisfaction, blame, and even more intense emotions such as self hate start chipping away, run a quick reality check. Those full hips? They bore a family. Those chubby thighs? They let you get up and dance. That bald head? It encases an intelligent and passionate mind.

HEARTBREAK

Cartoonist Lynda Barry calls love "an exploding cigar which we willingly smoke." Kaboom! The more you love, the worse you feel when it's gone. That's the blues, baby, and sooner or later everybody gets a serving of that messy gumbo of pain: rage and blame, jealousy and panic, spite, suspicion, despair.

Should I go on? While your heart is keening, call on your intelligence and intuition for some perspective. Intuition issues periodic accurate reports on the status of a relationship, but it's not unusual for emotional needs like *I need to be held, I want to be loved* to override the information. Take some time to listen to that inner voice. It will tell you if what you have is not worth keeping, if what you lost was no longer worth having.

Give yourself a side order of relief or acceptance with that gumbo. Then let your intelligence examine some of those needs. Your heart may not be able to distinguish between love and sex, but your brain can. Your heart may not be able to separate the vine-covered cottage of romance from the thorny reality of incompatibility, but your brain can. If heartbreak has become a pattern, call on your brain, intuition, and heart to examine the patterns of expectation that lead to it. And take Oprah's advice about failure: Try another path. Meanwhile, let go of that pain with feelings of self-respect, of gratitude for and generosity to the people in your life who love you no matter what.

"No one CAN MAKE YOU FEEL INFERIOR WITHOUT YOUR CONSENT"

—Eleanor Roosevelt

What wound did ever heal but by degree?

–Shakespeare

Mapping Your Emotional Self

You need
- a stack (30-50—you won't use them all the first time) of small paper squares
- a pen
- a quiet space to contemplate

Retire to that space with your materials. Sit comfortably, back straight, on the floor or in a chair. Close your eyes. Spend a few moments breathing and getting comfortable in your skin.

Now invite all your emotions to come to you. You don't have to be judgmental. Just write them down, one per square, as they arrive.* Start from your head where cool emotions reside, such as respect or spiritual devotion or ironic detachment. Move down to your throat to find expressive emotions, such as wonderment and happiness or the switch that turns on the silent treatment, and then down to your heart where warmer passions, such as love and gratitude—and the inability to accept them—reside. Continue to your lower torso, the source of ardent passions such as sexual desire, creativity, and jealousy,

* If you're at a loss for words to describe your feelings, turn back to the contrasting emotion lists on pages 21–25.

and the place where instinctive emotions such as suspicion and jealousy, but also a deep affinity for the earth, have a home.

Prepare to accept what you like along with what you don't, for it's human to be a patchwork of mixed emotions. Just follow the contours of your emotional self and write down the words that come to you. You may want to take several sittings to complete your map.

Now sift through the words and make two piles: the "positive" emotions and the "negative"emotions, according to how you feel about them. Note if the intensity of your emotions is strong (terror, rage, grief, for instance) or less so (such as anxiety, impatience, dissatisfaction). Notice if there is a preponderance of one particular type of emotion—fear, say. By the way, your words may be entirely different from mine.

Sit loosely in the saddle of life.

-Robert Louis Stevenson

Mapping your emotions is an exercise you can do over and over again. You may choose to do it at set intervals, perhaps every three months. Or on your birthday and half birthday. Or on the first day of each of the seasons.

Or you may choose to do it when a particular situation, person, or event in your life is troubling you. Perhaps you're looking to get along better with a co-worker who annoys you. Is the annoyance masking something else? Are you jealous? Or feeling inferior?

Perhaps you are mourning the end of a relationship. Or the end of a job. Use the Mapping Exercise to chart how you feel about this specific event or time in your life.

Keep the results in a notebook. As you track your changing emotional terrain, you'll begin to see what patterns emerge—rhythms of response to certain people or events and the intensity of your emotions. The point, of course, is not to eliminate the emotions from your life, but rather the situations that evince the emotions. As much as possible, be the observer as well as the participant—in essence integrating left brain and right brain, or head and heart. In this way, you embody both the map and the journey itself.

As you finish reading this section and move on to Part Two, allow yourself to think about which of the emotions you'd like to release and which you'd like to play a larger part in your life. Don't make this an intellectual exercise. Just let things percolate quietly at the nexus of mind and heart.

Better to be

without LOGIC

than

without FEELING.

–Charlotte Bronte, **The Professor**

Let It Go!

EVERYTHING

HAS AN

END.

—MASAI
SAYING

When you've mapped your emotional self and examined the results, you're ready to work on the next step: relinquishing each emotion in a situation that has caused you pain

You're not going to get over it. You're going to Let it Go. Because even if you surmount it, move past it, or just ignore it, it is still there just waiting for the opportunity to plant itself squarely in your path again. When you Let it Go, you release that negative issue through transformation. No more "it." Gone, sometimes literally into thin air.

For letting go in this transformational way, we look to Mother Earth, she of the wind, the tides, fire, regeneration, photosynthesis, oxidation, and all the cycles—day and night, growth and decay, the seasons—that have existed since our marvelous, self-sustaining blue-green orb took shape from a mass of gases eons ago.

Specifically, we look to the four elements—earth, fire, water, air—as the means through which we can transform the negative feelings in our lives into positive ones. As a guide to your transformation, you have at the back of this book a section of contracts to help you define your issues and direct them.

A Contract for Transformation

You will find 32 perforated fill-in-the-blank pages, eight for each of the four elements, to aid in your transformation. Think of each one as a ticket to the state you want to achieve, the person you want to be. Sounds simplistic, but filling in the blanks by naming your problem and directing yourself toward its resolution is the first step in making it so. Who else has the power to change your life but you?

Self-trust is the FIRST secret of success.

–Ralph Waldo Emerson

These contracts are yours to burn, shred, bury, flush, plant, crumple, fold, slice, stitch or otherwise invest with your energy, which in turn will guide you. You decide whether you want to enhance your contract with a related ritual or contemplation (suggested farther along in this section). Or simply speak your intent, which is, in essence, a meditation.

The more specific you can be about what you're feeling and why—and about what you want and how you'd like to feel— the better.

Here's how it works:

I *Joanna Arettam*

let go of *jealousy in my romantic relationship*

_____.

In shredding this paper, I commit to the purifying power of air all the negativity that has made me feel *cynical and untrusting*

_____.

As the tiny pieces are borne aloft by the wind, my own negative emotions are scattered so widely that they no longer exert control, leaving me with the opportunity for a fresh breath and a new, healthier way of living.

I make way for *intuition and resolve*

to come into my life. **Specific thoughts:**

With intuition——the wisdom of mind and heart—— as my guide, I will gather the strength to either embrace my relationship fully, letting go of the unwarranted jealousy that is holding me back, or opt out of a less-than-honest situation that does not offer the mutual love, trust, and respect necessary for a life together.

The Elements

The four elements are both physical and metaphysical. They are tangible and perceptible, of course, yet they are representative of particular states: solid, liquid, gas, and that which is transmuted before our eyes from one state to another. In their representative incarnation, the four elements are the essence of life itself. So we find them in metaphysical systems such as astrology and the chakras, in transformational volumes such as the *I Ching*, and in spiritual ceremonies that incorporate bathing, burning, chanting, and burying, each of which engages us in a particular way.

There's no one element or ritual that's best for transformation, only the one that resonates most fully for you at a particular time. For instance, a volatile emotion such as anger may call for an equally volatile transformative element, fire—the old flame-fighting-flame notion. And a deeply buried emotion such as sorrow may ask to be coaxed slowly via a more solid element such as earth. There is a nearly infinte combination of emotions and elements. Your personality or your issue will let you connect intuitively to the right combination for you.

LET IT GO WITH THE
NURTURING POWER OF EARTH

**Earth mother. . . You are the embrace
that heartens and the freedom beyond fear.**

—Starhawk

This element represents the solidity of terra firma, the safe bosom of Mother Nature. If you respond primally to the feeling of grass beneath your feet or dirt between your fingers, if you're a builder or a potter, if you're not afraid to roll up your sleeves and get your hands dirty, if Woodstock remains an ideal, this is your element. Would you rather drive than fly? Would you choose the mountains over the ocean? This is your element.

Are you a Taurus, Virgo, or Capricorn? You're an earth sign, so of course this is your element. If your style is slow and steady, if your temperament is rock solid, if you like having both feet on the ground, physically or otherwise, this is your element. Because negative emotions and situations are earth-shaking for you—you find it deeply unsettling when your psychological solid ground starts to crumble beneath your feet—earth-based transformations let you regain your footing.

If you feel that someone has been walking all over you or if you simply want to put down roots somewhere or with someone, you may want to incorporate transformative actions or rituals that involve the earth. Even mowing the lawn can be a contemplative—and thus transformative—action. And just think what it does for the lawn.

These deities may offer companionship or inspiration: Mother Earth in the Wiccan form of Gaia, the creator, who holds a shimmering turquoise sphere in her hands; the prehistoric Venus of Willendorf, whose ample proportions suggest the earth itself (and remind us that beauty comes in all sizes); Green Man, the forest god who represents the Druidic power and divinity of nature; Siddartha, an ordinary man who meditated on the ground under the leaves of the Bodhi tree until enlightenment came and he became the Buddha; Diana, the Roman hunter, the original woman who runs with the wolves.

 *Earth*

I _____

let go of_____.

In burying this paper, I commit to the healing, powerful earth all the
negativity that has made me feel_____

_____.

As the paper decays into the soil, my own negative feelings decompose
into a fertile emotional mulch that will propagate a new, healthier way of living.

I make way for_____
to come into my life.

When you're ready to let go of something by burying it,
turn to the earth contracts at the end of this book.

A Ritual for Letting Go

Burying is an act whose effect is carried out over time. When someone you love dies, interment is the last step in the ritual of grieving, but the first step in the long-term process of coming to terms with the death. So, too, is the burying of your contract. The emotions and situations represented on your contract will disintegrate over time if you will it to be so. In the meantime, planting seeds or bulbs will yield a tangible reminder of the beauty that can come into your life. Place a handful of potting soil into a vessel, or even better, a garden plot. Set your list—crumpled, folded, shredded, whatever feels right to you—into the soil, covering it with more soil. Now set a bulb or seeds on top of that and cover it with soil, saying or thinking words such as these (I'm using anger as the example):

I bury my anger so that the earth may transform it. As I resolve the situations that have created anger in me, I know it's OK to express my feelings in clear, certain terms, but I will not dump my rage on anyone else. And I will not bury it inside myself. I plant these seeds as an act of change, to create a new life without just as I will create a new life within.

Consider that negative emotions about family, about property, or about home, food, and income spring from the tribal, primal self—our inner cavewoman or caveman, so to speak. The positive need to feel grounded springs from that same primal place. You may incorporate these rituals—or others of your own making—with your contract.

Get out of the car. Take a walk or a hike or go barefoot on the grass. Visit a temple, church, or shrine, being aware that current buildings are often built on or over earlier structures that were placed on land divined to be sacred; you don't have to pray in any traditional way, just let the powerful energy of the space enter your physical body, from the soles of your feet to the top of your head, while releasing through your breath the negative energy that has been holding you back.

Mother Earth, I am your child. I open myself to your life-giving power. I seek to heal and be whole.

Allow me to unburden myself to you so that the seeds of what is healthy and strong within me can take root and grow.

$\mathcal{S}$culpt clay, carve wood, create a rock collection, plant a vegetable garden, arrange flowers. Interacting physically with the earth in expressive ways such as these is a reminder that creativity, like life itself, is not simply about imposing your will on your subject but allowing yourself to recognize and accept the inspiration suggested by the medium.

I push, you yield. You push, I push back. Push, yield, push, yield. Sometimes we relax into each other. How like dancing (or making love) it is to create with the fruits of your physical self. Working with and through you I relinquish what troubles me. I feel grounded, centered. I am whole.

$\mathcal{S}$ay a grace with your meal. Food is the ultimate physical transformation. The seed yields a plant; the plant, a meal; the meal becomes you. For this reason, women in the pre-Islamic, pre-Judeo-Christian Middle East worshipped the goddess Asherah, creating loaves of bread in her image, a ritual that was transformed centuries later into the Christian sacrament of Holy Communion. This is a particularly resonant contemplation if issues about weight, body image, or food are holding you back.

Thank you for this abundance of healthy food and for the taste buds that make consuming it so enjoyable. Sometimes I come to the table with a hunger that food alone cannot satisfy. Mother Earth, help me distinguish between what I'm eating and what's eating me, so that I can properly nourish my body and my spirit in equal measure. And with equal pleasure.

Let It Go with the Transformative Power of Fire

Fire is a good companion for the mind.

—May Sarton

Are you an Aries, Leo or Sagittarius? You're a fire sign and very likely drawn to the heat or light of a flame. Fire has enormous power. Though devastating when out of control, it can be used to clear brush and fertilize the soil when restrained, and, when harnessed, provide us with the most basic of creature comforts: heat, light and a cooking flame. Those for whom this element resonates may be drawn to its power of destruction or of nurturance or perhaps to issues that involve both. So, whatever your sign, you of the volatile emotions, the incandescent laugh, the burning passion, the warm personality, the warrior spirit, or the red hair: this is your element.

Fire is a powerful element for transformation because its nature is to create change. Around a hearth, you can watch wood turn to ash, warming you in the process. Fire combines with the other elements: with earth, in the firing of clay or the baking of bread (grains are harvested from the earth), or with air, which fuels the flames; it even combines with water to make steam, and if you've ever spent time in a sweat lodge or steamroom, you know how physically transformative water vapor can be. If you are in a period of emotional flux or if situations around you are changing in ways that affect your stability, you may want to redirect that mutability through focused actions involving this element. Let's not overlook the intense emotionality of a fiery temper or smoldering resentment. Isn't it time to let them burn out in a way that doesn't burn you out?

Deities who may resonate for you include Chango, the god of fire and lightning in Afro-Cuban Santeria, whose attributes are power and passion; Shiva, the Hindu lord of life, dancing divinely within his circle of flame, or Kali, the goddess of destruction and creation who purges us of fear, anger, jealousy, and grief; Zeus, the ruler of Mount Olympus, or his daughter, the powerful Athena, who sprang in a bolt of lightning from his head to serve as an inspiration for independence for us all; Eros, the Greek god who fans the flames of love and romance.

Fire

I _____

let go of _____.

In burning this paper, I commit to the transformative power of flame all the negativity that has made me feel _____

_____.

As the paper turns to ash, its energy is released into the universe. Similarly, as my negative emotions combust harmlessly, their energy will fuel a new, healthier way of living.

I make way for _____

to come into my life.

When you're ready to let go by burning away some part of your life, turn to the fire contracts at the end of this book.

A Ritual for Letting Go

In burning your contract, you will bid farewell to all the pain you have borne within you. Set a small votive candle into a sturdy ceramic vessel. Light it. Tear off the corner of your contract, offering it carefully to the flame, then continue piece by piece until the contract has been consumed. (If you are doing this out of doors, you can burn the entire page with one dramatic flourish.) As you do, say or think words such as these (I'm using fear as the example) *I feed this flame with a contract that represents the fear that has been consuming me. What a relief to watch it go up in smoke! With the help of a benevolent universe and my own burning desire, I invite courage into my life.*

The transformative power of fire and heat can inspire many ways for you to transform your own life. It is particularly effective for issues involving burning passion—anger, jealousy, smoldering resentment—and romance, from delirium at the first spark to heartbreak at the dying embers.

Focus on the flame. As a prelude to meditation, a candle flame can help you focus your energy. However, it can also be part of a simple ritual for letting go, particularly if what you want to release are anxiety and the tensions of day-to-day life. Take 10 minutes. In a darkened room, light a candle and sit quietly before it. With each exhalation, expel the negative energy you have generated or attracted during the day. Imagine that energy being consumed by the flame.

From the jumble of activity that has shaped my day, I retreat here to a single point of light in the darkness. How calming is its steady flame. With each breath out, I release the anxiety I have carried within me. With each breath in, I gratefully receive tranquility to take its place.

Amplify your creative energy with fire and heat. You've probably noticed that your problems retreat to the back of your mind when your imagination is engaged. That's because creativity is a wellspring of positive energy. As you glaze your pot before putting it into the kiln, as you solder metal into jewelry, as you knead bread or assemble your ingredients for the preparation of a meal, recognize the buoyant spirit you bring to the act and allow it to enter the object of your creation.

My creativity is rich and joyful. I offer this energy to the pot (bracelet, bread, meal) before me, knowing that just as fire and heat transform materials from raw to finished, my own good spirits will be forged into a more durable state—so that they will always be there for me when I need them.

Engage the purgative power of fire. Build a small bonfire to let you clear your life not just of the feelings but of the actual objects that have held you back. Old photographs? Love letters? Toss them in. What better way is there to let go of an old flame! Maybe you'll save things to be burned at the winter solstice, when the year comes to an end. Have you had a difficult year? Burn the calendar page by page, reflecting on each issue that has held you back—perhaps identifying the emotion out loud as you bid it a transformative farewell. Add a sprig of purifying sage to prepare a path for the future.

I cast this object to the flames to release the passion I've carried for _____. I wish him (her) no harm, only a swift retreat from my heart. As I relinquish the past and look to the future, I will for myself—right here, right now—the strength to be open to a new love and the intuition to recognize if it is not right for me.

LET IT GO WITH THE
CLEANSING POWER OF WATER
....

The sea, the ever renewing sea!

—Charmes

We cannot but have a primordial connection to this element. Our bodies, which developed in a uterine sea of amniotic fluid, are mostly water and minerals, like the ocean itself. While the power of rushing river torrents and crashing ocean waves can be formidable, their steady currents and rhymthic tides are a regulating force for our planet and in our lives. Water cleanses the body, and in virtually all cultures it is employed ritually to cleanse the soul—from a sprinkle of holy water over the forehead in a Christian baptism to a full-body immersion in the Hindu's sacred Ganges. If you are a water sign—Cancer, Scorpio, or Pisces; a swimmer; someone who has chosen to make a career in, on, or around the water; or if you have chosen to live or spend time near a body of water, you are drawn to the transformative, especially healing, aspect of this element. In fact, recreation and renewal are often one and the same for you.

Want to come clean? Whatever your sign or inclination, you will find that water is the one you can count on to wash away what troubles you. If you have psychic abilities, you may find them amplified near the water. And as any nurturer can tell you, water is the element that makes things grow. The change created by water is both swift—the way a swollen river tears away chunks of its bank—and interminably slow, the way a steady drip, drip, drip wears down rock over the ages. As you employ this element to release what's holding you back, reflect on whether the change you seek be speedy or gradual and create a ritual whose pulse is in tune with the momentum.

You may look to deities such as Kuan Yin, the Chinese goddess of compassion, who offers to those who seek it the serenity of a deep, cool lake; the Santeria orisha Yemaya, ruler of the ocean and the power that springs from it; the Christian Virgin Mary, whose blue robes evoke the sea as well as the heavens (now worshipped as the Mother of God, but who evolved from a long line of all-powerful matriarchial creators); Roman Venus, who emerged from the primordial foam to bring beauty and harmony to Earth.

Water

I _____

let go of _____.

In flushing this paper, I submit to the cleansing power of water all the negativity that has made me feel _____

_____.

As the fiber bonds of the paper begin to dissolve and are carried away, my own negative emotions soften and vanish, leaving in their wake the path for a new, healthier way of living.

I make way for _____

to come into my life

When you're ready to dissolve away a negativity,
turn to the water contracts at the end of this book.

A Ritual for Letting Go

Water covers over 75 percent of our planet. When you commit your contract to this element, you are diluting and transmuting whatever is holding you back. That's true whether you toss your contract into the ocean, drop it into a stream or flush it down the toilet. Water is so fluid that what was once vapor from your breath entered the atmosphere to become a cloud, which fell as rain and watered a plant that someone else ate, whose cells were hydrated and who exhaled water vapor that became a cloud that fell into the ocean that created fog that covered the land that was inhaled by thousands of people along the coast, and so on and so forth. So if you think you're alone with your pain, forget it. You're sharing it, literally with every breath. Cast your contract upon the water saying or thinking words such as these (I'm using self-hatred as the example): *I dissolve my self-hatred in the water, an entity so vast that even my enormous reservoir of pain cannot pollute it. All water eventually makes its way to the ocean, and the tide will carry my self-hatred into its depths, where currents will disperse it harmlessly into seas and into clouds, and into rivers and eventually back into my own bath. Happy in my own skin, I will slip contentedly into the water.*

ACTIVE CONTEMPLATIONS FOR LETTING GO

Yes, water is healing and ritually symbolic of transformation, but it's also fun and sybaritic. You can tap into those aspects when you make way for change in your life.

Dive in. The celebration of a new spiritual life is often carried out with the sprinkling of or full immersion in water. When you decide to let go of the issues that hold you back, you are creating your life and spirit anew. Instead of a baptism in the traditional sense, experience water in a different way: If you're a swimmer, go water skiing; if you're a snorkeler, run through a sprinkler; if you're a diver, take a walk in the rain; if you're the sort who prefers to sit by a lake, well, dive in. When you see—and feel—water from a different perspective, it's a short, creative leap to looking for and experiencing new aspects of your life.

Inside, outside. Over and through. In the spirit of transformation, I seek to experience in a new way this element that is so familiar to me. I'm curious. Although I may be tentative I'm not afraid, for I am buoyant and I know how to swim. In the same spirit, I immerse myself joyfully in the ocean of life. I will not be overcome, for I am resilient. I know how to live.

Send a message in a bottle. Don't keep those negative feeling stopped up inside. Instead, on a slip of paper write down what's bothering you—words, phrases, a short poem, whatever expresses how you feel—and drop it into a bottle. When the bottle is full, cast it to the elements. (If launching a bottle into the water runs counter to your ecological sensibilities, just recycle it. The making of the list and the contemplation of its contents are more important than the means of conveyance.) You'll adapt this contemplation to your specific situation.

Anger, your furious words and acrimonious feelings have exploded out of me for the last time; there is no room for you in my life. Jealousy, you have ruled my heart for too long; it's time to go. Anxiety,

I'm no longer touched by your vague and unsettled stirrings; good-bye. I cast you out of my life knowing your power will diminish to nothing.

Make yourself a cup of tea. Not in a teapot. In a tub. You're the teabag, releasing into the steamy water all the negative emotions you may be feeling. Just lie there and steep. Add real herbs or teabags to the tub and you'll be infused with an aromatic sense of well-being. Try Camomile, Valerian, or St. John's Wort for relaxation; ginger, ginseng, or peppermint to rejuvenate.

Instead of brooding in unhappiness, I'm steeping in pleasure. I can feel my disappointment seep out of every pore, my muscles softening in direct proportion to the emotional toxins leaving my body. Down the drain you go, dejection. I am washed clean.

Let It Go with the Purifying Power of Air

. . . .

. . . the air has resurrection in it.

–Eugene de Guerin

Mercury, the winged messenger, is your archetype. You're the one who communicates nimbly with song, image, or word, the one who moves with a bounce to your step, as if you're being borne aloft by the breeze. Sometimes you feel as if you could walk on air. You don't need to be a Gemini, Libra, or Aquarius to feel drawn to this element. Whatever your zodiacal sign or interest, your inclination is to live life unfettered so issues that tie you down spiritually or emotionally are especially vexing. Simply put: You need room to breathe.

Air is mightily transformative. It's the least tangible of the four elements yet without air the others are not complete: it's the O (oxygen) of H_2O; the atmospheric nimbus that cloaks our Earth; the fuel that ignites the flame. If air is your element, you may feel a bit like that yourself occasionally: essential yet overlooked. In the best of times, your vigor is sought out and your effort praised; in the worst of times, it is the self-defeating energy of the enabler. You, more than the others, need to air out what's bothering you through talking, chanting, singing. Spend some contemplative time out of doors, particularly in wide-open spaces. You might also consider pranayama yoga, conscious breathing that lets the prana, or life force of the universe, into the universe within yourself.

As you peer within for inspiration, you may want to look heavenward as well: to Winged Isis, the Oldest of the Old in ancient Egypt, who caught the souls of the departed in her wings and bore them to eternal life; Oya, the Yoruba orisha of wind, who offers us the gift of breath; the glorious, powerful Amazons who sent arrows through the air; Saraswati, the Hindu goddess of art, language, music, and creative energy. Or consider the eagle. A totem of power for many Native American tribes, it has the ability to soar into the realm of the spirit, yet it always returns to earth—a reminder to all that letting go does not mean giving up.

 *Air*

I _____

let go of _____.

In shredding this paper, I commit to the puryifying power of air all the
negativity that has made me feel _____

_____.

As the tiny pieces are borne aloft by the wind, my own negative emotions
are scattered so widely that they no longer exert control, leaving me with the
opportunity for a fresh breath and new, healthier way of living.

I make way for _____

to come into my life.

When you're ready to release a negativity,
turn to the air contracts at the end of this book.

A Ritual for Letting Go

To scatter your contract, get yourself to a wide-open space—a rolling meadow, for instance, or a bluff overlooking the ocean where you'll inhale plenty of good negative ions with the salty breeze. Part of your ritual is to take yourself away from the environment that constricts you. Physically, you need a breath of fresh air, because in shouldering your emotional burden, you have not allowed your lungs to expand to their fullest. Sighs, after all, are the body's attempt to get air deeply into the lungs. As you disperse your contract, say or think words such as these (I'm using sadness as the example): *I cast my sadness to the air so that the wind may carry it far from me, and in so many pieces that it can never return. To bring lightness to my heavy heart, I breathe in the expansiveness of the universe, knowing that its power—and my own desire to be free—will ease and disperse my pain.*

Active Contemplations for Letting Go

With each breath, we take in the power of the universe. The Yogis call it prana, the energy that gives life to all things. With air as your transformative element, you are particularly receptive to rituals and activities that involve voice, vibration, and communication.

Sing aloud. Pop in a favorite CD and croon away. Singing feels good because your entire torso is involved in the song: your diaphragm vibrates, your lungs fill and empty fully, and the muscles in your throat and mouth experience a full range of motion. You are the harmonic expression of yin and yang. While you're at it, clap your hands, wave your arms, dance. It's no coincidence that singing and dancing are essential elements in the rituals of worship and ecstasy in cultures around the world. You don't need a contemplation here—just open your mouth and sing—but if you want one, try this:

My heart is open to the hearts of all beings. My spirit is open to the infinity of the universe. I am a radio antenna tuned into the divine, and my song is its joyful expression.

Chant. Chanting is the ascetic form of singing—more focused and thus more intense. The repetitive nature of chanting encourages rhythmic breathing, and that in turn fosters a sense of physical calm while increasing spiritual energy. It is an excellent means of transforming negative energy and letting it out of your life. Different chants have different vibrations, each of which affects the mind and body in a different way. Look for a chanting group or even a CD to find the vibrations that resonate most fully for you. Create a time each day when you can retire to a quiet place, sit comfortably and chant. In the meantime, call upon the power of the universe by saying its name: Aum. Intone it in one breath, repeating it as often as you wish:

Aaaaaaaaaaahhhhhhhhhh-ooooooooooooo-mmmmmmmm.

Have a heart-to-heart talk with someone.

Sometimes we clam up when we are most in need of conversation. The contemplation below will help you summon the power to reach out. With that power, all you have to do is pick up the phone, log on to the Internet or, here's a low-tech option, drop in on a friend for a chat.

There is so much I need to get off my chest. I will begin by taking a deep, liberating breath. And another. With each inhalation and exhalation, I feel my lungs claim their rightful space within my ribcage, relaxing the muscles that band my chest. With each inhalation and exhalation, I feel my throat muscles soften. With each inhalation and exhalation, I open a space for that verbal extension of myself, my voice.

Beyond the Four Elements: Four Simple Words

I'm sorry. I forgive.

In relationships you inflict or receive pain—sometimes intentionally in a preemptive strike, more often unintentionally when mixed signals or misinterpreted motives get in the way of communication. Contrition and forgiveness are profound acts that amplify your efforts to let go of negativity. Accept them into your life. Use them often. Embrace them as mantras. Give them as gifts. Acknowledge them as the Twin Towers of release and repair, for they are the basis of all change for the better. These towers have been standing since the dawn of humanity. They will not fall.

"I have been in sorrow's kitchen and licked all the pots. Then I have stood on the peaky mountain wrapped in rainbows, with a harp and sword in my hand."

—ZORA NEALE HURSTON,
DUST TRACKS ON A ROAD

There came a time when the **risk** to remain tight in the **bud** was more painful than the risk it took to **blossom**.

—Anaïs Nin

part three

The Contracts

Contracts for Transformation

Change is good. Focused change is better. And intuitively directed change is best of all. There's no situation too small to warrant your attention or too large to be effected. On the small side, for instance, you could carry out a ritual when you get home from work each evening to mark the transformation of energy from your "work" self to your "home" self and, not incidentally, eliminate the tension you have carried all day. On the big side, there are the life-altering changes you must make when anger or grief are so rooted in your being that they block out all other emotions. (You may want to tackle a big issue all at once, or approach it day by day to work your transformation over time.)

Remember, there's no one "right way" to effect your transformation. Tap your intuition to help you choose which element you need for your particular emotion at a particular time. What element do you feel like today? Sometimes the simple act of sitting quietly for a moment will allow the appropriate path to open up to you.

Use these Contracts for Transformation to release emotional pain and make way for the life you've always wanted.

earth

I _____
let go of _____

In burying this paper, I commit to the healing, powerful earth all the negativity
that has made me feel _____.

As the paper decays into the soil, my own negative feelings decompose into a
fertile emotional mulch that will propagate a new, healthier way of living.

I make way for _____
to come into my life.

Earth

I _____

let go of _____

In burying this paper, I commit to the healing, powerful earth all the negativity that has made me feel _____ .

As the paper decays into the soil, my own negative feelings decompose into a fertile emotional mulch that will propagate a new, healthier way of living.

I make way for _____

to come into my life.

earth

I _____

let go of _____
_____ .

In burying this paper, I commit to the healing, powerful earth all the negativity that has made me feel _____
_____ .

As the paper decays into the soil, my own negative feelings decompose into a fertile emotional mulch that will propagate a new, healthier way of living.

I make way for _____
to come into my life.

earth

I _____

let go of _____

In burying this paper, I commit to the healing powerful earth all the negativity

that has made me feel _____

As the paper decays into the soil, my own negative feelings decompose into a

fertile emotional mulch that will propagate a new, healthier way of living.

I make way for _____

to come into my life.

earth

I _____

let go of _____

In burying this paper, I commit to the healing, powerful earth all the negativity
that has made me feel _____.

As the paper decays into the soil, my own negative feelings decompose into a
fertile emotional mulch that will propagate a new, healthier way of living.

I make way for _____

to come into my life.

earth

I

let go of _____

_____

In burying this paper, I commit to the healing, powerful earth all the negativity

that has made me feel _____ .

As the paper decays into the soil, my own negative feelings decompose into a

fertile emotional mulch that will propagate a new, healthier way of living.

I make way for _____

to come into my life.

Earth

I _____

let go of _____

In burying this paper, I commit to the healing, powerful earth all the negativity that has made me feel _____.

As the paper decays into the soil, my own negative feelings decompose into a fertile emotional mulch that will propagate a new, healthier way of living.

I make way for _____

to come into my life.

earth

I _____

let go of _____

_____.

In burying this paper, I commit to the healing, powerful earth all the negativity

that has made me feel _____

_____.

As the paper decays into the soil, my own negative feelings decompose into a

fertile emotional mulch that will propagate a new, healthier way of living.

I make way for _____

to come into my life.

Fire

I

let go of _____

_____ .

In burning this paper, I yield to the transformative power of flame all the

negativity that has made me feel _____

_____ .

As the paper turns to ash, its energy is released into the universe. Similarly,

as my negative emotions combust harmlessly, their energy will fuel a new,

healthier way of living.

I make way for _____

to come into my life.

Fire

I _____ let go of _____

In burning this paper, I yield to the transformative power of flame all the negativity that has made me feel _____.

As the paper turns to ash, its energy is released into the universe. Similarly, as my negative emotions combust harmlessly, their energy will fuel a new, healthier way of living.

I make way for _____ to come into my life.

Fire

I _____ let go of _____ .

In burning this paper, I yield to the transformative power of flame all the

negativity that has made me feel _____

_____ .

As the paper turns to ash, its energy is released into the universe. Similarly,

as my negative emotions combust harmlessly, their energy will fuel a new,

healthier way of living.

I make way for _____

to come into my life.

Fire

I _____

let go of _____

In burning this paper, I yield to the transformative power of flame all the

negativity that has made me feel _____

As the paper turns to ash, its energy is released into the universe. Similarly,

as my negative emotions combust harmlessly, their energy will fuel a new,

healthier way of living.

I make way for _____

to come into my life.

Fire

I _____
let go of _____
_____.

In burning this paper, I yield to the transformative power of flame all the

negativity that has made me feel _____

_____.

As the paper turns to ash, its energy is released into the universe. Similarly,

as my negative emotions combust harmlessly, their energy will fuel a new,

healthier way of living.

I make way for _____

to come into my life.

Fire

I _____

let go of _____

In burning this paper, I yield to the transformative power of flame all the

negativity that has made me feel _____

_____ .

As the paper turns to ash, its energy is released into the universe. Similarly,

as my negative emotions combust harmlessly, their energy will fuel a new,

healthier way of living.

I make way for _____

to come into my life.

Fire

I _____
let go of _____

In burning this paper, I yield to the transformative power of flame all the
negativity that has made me feel _____ .

As the paper turns to ash, its energy is released into the universe. Similarly,
as my negative emotions combust harmlessly, their energy will fuel a new,
healthier way of living.

I make way for _____
to come into my life.

Fire

I
let go of _____

_____

In burning this paper, I yield to the transformative power of flame all the

negativity that has made me feel _____

_____.

As the paper turns to ash, its energy is released into the universe. Similarly,

as my negative emotions combust harmlessly, their energy will fuel a new,

healthier way of living.

I make way for _____

to come into my life.

Water

I let go of _____

In flushing this paper, I submit to the cleansing power of water all the negativity that has made me feel _____.

As the fiber bonds of the paper begin to dissolve and are carried away, my own negative emotions soften and vanish, leaving in their wake the path for a new, healthier way of living.

I make way for _____ to come into my life.

Water

I _____

let go of _____

   In flushing this paper, I submit to the cleansing power of water all the

negativity that has made me feel _____

_____.

   As the fiber bonds of the paper begin to dissolve and are carried away, my

own negative emotions soften and vanish, leaving in their wake the path for a

new, healthier way of living.

   I make way for _____

to come into my life.

Water

I

let go of _____.

   In flushing this paper, I submit to the cleansing power of water all the negativity that has made me feel _____.

   As the fiber bonds of the paper begin to dissolve and are carried away, my own negative emotions soften and vanish, leaving in their wake the path for a new, healthier way of living.

   I make way for _____

to come into my life.

Water

I _____

let go of _____

In flushing this paper, I submit to the cleansing power of water all the

negativity that has made me feel _____.

As the fiber bonds of the paper begin to dissolve and are carried away, my

own negative emotions soften and vanish, leaving in their wake the path for a

new, healthier way of living.

I make way for _____

to come into my life.

Water

I let go of _____

In flushing this paper, I submit to the cleansing power of water all the negativity that has made me feel _____.

As the fiber bonds of the paper begin to dissolve and are carried away, my own negative emotions soften and vanish, leaving in their wake the path for a new, healthier way of living.

I make way for _____ to come into my life.

Water

I

let go of _____

In flushing this paper, I submit to the cleansing power of water all the

negativity that has made me feel _____.

As the fiber bonds of the paper begin to dissolve and are carried away, my

own negative emotions soften and vanish, leaving in their wake the path for a

new, healthier way of living.

I make way for _____

to come into my life.

Water

I _____
let go of _____

In flushing this paper, I submit to the cleansing power of water all the
negativity that has made me feel _____.

As the fiber bonds of the paper begin to dissolve and are carried away, my
own negative emotions soften and vanish, leaving in their wake the path for a
new, healthier way of living.

I make way for _____
to come into my life.

Water

I _____
let go of _____.

In flushing this paper, I submit to the cleansing power of water all the negativity that has made me feel _____.

As the fiber bonds of the paper begin to dissolve and are carried away, my own negative emotions soften and vanish, leaving in their wake the path for a new, healthier way of living.

I make way for _____
to come into my life.

Air

I _____

let go of _____

In shredding this paper, I commit to the puryifying power of air all the

negativity that has made me feel _____

_____.

As the tiny pieces are borne aloft by the wind, my own negative emotions
are scattered so widely that they no longer exert control, leaving me with the
opportunity for a fresh breath and a new, healthier way of living.

I make way for _____

to come into my life.

Air

I _____

let go of _____

In shredding this paper, I commit to the puryifying power of air all the

negativity that has made me feel _____

_____ .

As the tiny pieces are borne aloft by the wind, my own negative emotions

are scattered so widely that they no longer exert control, leaving me with the

opportunity for a fresh breath and a new, healthier way of living.

I make way for _____

to come into my life.

Air

I _____

let go of _____

_____

In shredding this paper, I commit to the puryifying power of air all the

negativity that has made me feel _____

_____

As the tiny pieces are borne aloft by the wind, my own negative emotions

are scattered so widely that they no longer exert control, leaving me with the

opportunity for a fresh breath and a new, healthier way of living.

I make way for _____

to come into my life.

Air

I
let go of _____.

In shredding this paper, I commit to the puryifying power of air all the

negativity that has made me feel _____.

As the tiny pieces are borne aloft by the wind, my own negative emotions

are scattered so widely that they no longer exert control, leaving me with the

opportunity for a fresh breath and a new, healthier way of living.

I make way for _____

to come into my life.

Air

I

let go of _____

_____

In shredding this paper, I commit to the puryifying power of air all the

negativity that has made me feel _____

_____

As the tiny pieces are borne aloft by the wind, my own negative emotions

are scattered so widely that they no longer exert control, leaving me with the

opportunity for a fresh breath and a new, healthier way of living.

I make way for _____

to come into my life.

Air

I _____

let go of _____

In shredding this paper, I commit to the purifying power of air all the

negativity that has made me feel _____ .

As the tiny pieces are borne aloft by the wind, my own negative emotions

are scattered so widely that they no longer exert control, leaving me with the

opportunity for a fresh breath and a new, healthier way of living.

I make way for _____

to come into my life.

Air

I _____

let go of _____

In shredding this paper, I commit to the puryifying power of air all the negativity that has made me feel _____

negativity that has made me feel _____

As the tiny pieces are borne aloft by the wind, my own negative emotions are scattered so widely that they no longer exert control, leaving me with the opportunity for a fresh breath and a new, healthier way of living.

I make way for _____

to come into my life.

air

I _____

let go of _____ .

In shredding this paper, I commit to the puryifying power of air all the

negativity that has made me feel _____ .

As the tiny pieces are borne aloft by the wind, my own negative emotions
are scattered so widely that they no longer exert control, leaving me with the
opportunity for a fresh breath and a new, healthier way of living.

I make way for _____

to come into my life.